HOW Mother Nature GOT HER JOB

By Suzanne Weyn
Illustrated by Wendy Rasmussen

Modern Curriculum Press
Parsippany, New Jersey

1-800-321-3106
www.pearsonlearning.com

Contents

For darling, dear Rae Gonzalez

Chapter 1

Some Excitement at Last

I didn't want to spend the summer in the country. I was used to living in the city. There were bright lights and big sounds in the city. Tall buildings were crowded together on every street, and there were people everywhere.

My name is Sam. This is the story of how a summer that might have been dull turned into the most amazing vacation I ever had.

My Aunt Susana's house is a hundred years old and stuck in the middle of nowhere. That's where my parents thought I would have fun, so that summer I was stuck in the middle of nowhere, too.

In the country it was quiet. Crickets and birds were all I could hear. It was strange. There weren't even any other people! The only nearby house was down the hill and across the road, and no one even lived there. It was empty.

I might have gone crazy from boredom if it wasn't for my cousin Rae. Rae's great. The first week I was there, we rode our bikes a lot and went exploring. I had never seen so many trees in one place before. There was a park near my apartment at home, but even it didn't have as many trees as Aunt Sue's big backyard.

One afternoon, Rae and I were on the porch.
We were watching a spider make a huge web
under the railing. As we watched, a car headed
down the road. It was the first car I'd seen come
down that road all week. I didn't count Aunt
Sue's car because she lived here. This was a
new person, someone I'd never seen before.

"Oh!" Rae cried. Her eyes got wide as she stared at the car. "This is great!"

Rae and I had been waiting for something exciting to happen. Still, it was just a car. "What's so great about seeing a car?" I asked.

"That's not just any car," Rae replied.

The car stopped in front of the old house across the road. I was too far away to see who got out of the car. Rae bounded off the porch, and moving fast, she ran down the hill.

I couldn't understand why Rae was so excited. On the other hand, I didn't have anything else to do, so I decided to follow Rae.

Rae had a head start, but I caught up to her at the bottom of the walkway. By now a woman had gotten out of the car.

"Hi," Rae called over to the woman. The woman waved.

Rae turned toward me, a big smile on her face. "She saw me! She waved!" she said. "Oh, I love it when she's home. She's so great. Wait until you meet her. Just wait!"

Opening the back of the car, the woman pulled out something large and flat.

I frowned, puzzled. Why was Rae so excited about this lady? "Who is she?" I asked.

"It's Demeter Dunn," Rae told me, as if this was something everyone knew except me. "When Demeter Dunn is here, there's one thing you can always count on. Expect the unexpected!"

Chapter 2

The Visit

"Who is Demeter Dunn?" I asked. I had never heard of her before.

"She's a painter, a famous painter," Rae explained. "Her paintings are in art galleries and museums all over the world. She comes here when she wants to be alone to paint. Let's go visit her."

"You just said she comes here to be alone," I
reminded her.

"Oh, it's OK," Rae said as she crossed the
road. "She likes me. Come on!" It was
something to do, so I followed her.

Demeter Dunn took more and more flat
things out of the back of her car. As I got closer,
I could see that the flat things were paintings.

"Hi, Rae," she said when we reached her.
"Who's your friend?"

"This is Sam," Rae told her. "He's my cousin from the city."

Demeter looked me over. "I'm from the city, too. How do you like country life so far, Sam?" she asked.

"I'm having a good time, but it's kind of quiet," I answered.

Demeter grinned. "Right now I need country quiet for painting. I have a big art show coming up in two weeks, and I have to frame all of these paintings and paint one more."

We helped her carry the paintings into her house. Inside Demeter leaned the paintings against the walls and furniture so we could see. The paintings were sort of strange.

"I work in a style called abstract," she explained. "I try to capture the energy of life. Look at this one," Demeter said, pointing to a painting of colorful swirls. "It's a seed starting to burst open. I used bright colors and bold brush strokes to show the excitement."

"They're great!" Rae raved.

I couldn't figure them out. These paintings didn't look like any paintings I'd ever seen before. They weren't really pictures of anything.

"The colors are nice," I said, trying to be polite to Demeter.

Demeter laughed. "I know it doesn't look like a seed," she said. "It's not supposed to. It's supposed to give you the feeling of a seed."

Hmmmm, I thought.

Rae and I left Demeter alone to finish unpacking, and we went back to our positions on the porch, watching the spider web.

The next morning, Rae suggested we visit
Demeter again.

"She's busy," I reminded her.

"I know," Rae admitted with a sigh. "We won't
stay long."

After breakfast we headed over to Demeter
Dunn's house. As we neared the road, Rae
suddenly stopped and turned her head sharply.
She had heard something, and I heard it, too.
Then it came swinging around the corner and
we both saw it.

Chapter 3

A Twister Blows Through

Another car we had never seen before was coming down the road. This car was a big, old-fashioned, pink convertible with the top down. The horn blasted as it sped toward us.

As the car passed us, we could see a woman driving. Her long white hair whipped around her face in the breeze.

The car came to a sudden stop in front of
Demeter's house, and the driver hopped out.
Her long dress flapped in a sudden wind.

Her hair was messy and wind-blown when she
got out of the car. Then, as she moved around
the car, something funny happened. Her hair
smoothed down almost as if an invisible comb
had fixed it.

The woman pulled an enormous suitcase out
of the backseat. It looked heavy, but she lifted it
with no problem. Then she skipped up the front
steps and right into Demeter's house. She didn't
even ring the doorbell!

Rae and I looked at each other. Who was this
lady? What was going on?

We walked around the car. The backseat was jammed full of stuff. There were more gigantic suitcases. There were also some potted plants, two birdcages with birds in them, and a goldfish bowl with two goldfish. There was even a big, furry rabbit calmly sitting in a baby seat.

"It looks as if the lady is moving," Rae said, "or else going on a very long vacation."

"We'd better leave," I said. "Demeter has company." Rae nodded and we turned to go.

Suddenly a strong wind whipped my hair. A funnel-shaped cloud twirled through Demeter's yard. It looked like a miniature tornado. Rae stumbled as it spun around her.

The little tornado moved on, spinning right into Demeter's kitchen window. A few minutes later the strange woman came out. This time she didn't have the suitcase. Her snowy white hair was blowing wildly again, but she didn't seem to care.

Then the lady did a funny trick. She didn't open the car door. Instead she took a running leap and dove over the back. One minute she was flying through the air in a somersault. The next minute she was sitting behind the wheel. Turning toward us, she winked and waved. We jumped away from the car as she started it up.

The wind suddenly stopped. We could hear the woman blasting her car stereo and singing along loudly as she zoomed off. As she drove away, I noticed she had an unusual license plate. It said H2O'N'O2. I knew H_2O stood for water and O_2 stood for oxygen. Water and oxygen was a strange thing to have on a license plate.

"Let's see if Demeter is OK!" Rae cried.

We rushed inside. Demeter's house sure looked like a storm had hit it. Papers had blown everywhere, the furniture was crooked, and lampshades tilted crazily.

"Demeter!" Rae called as we hurried through the house. "Where are you?"

"In here," Demeter's dazed voice came from the kitchen.

"Oh!" Rae gasped when she saw her.

Demeter's hair was sticking straight up in the air. Her robe was on backwards. Her slippers were even on the wrong feet!

"Who was that woman?" I asked.

Demeter blinked. She looked as if she couldn't believe what had just happened. "That was Mother Nature," she answered.

"Mother who?" Rae asked.

"Nature. Mother Nature," Demeter repeated. "I've never seen that woman before, but that's who she told me she was. The moment she said it, that crazy tornado blew through."

"We saw it," Rae said. "It headed right in your window as if it knew where it was going."

Demeter nodded slowly. "She said it was time for her to retire. She said I had been chosen as the new Mother Nature," Demeter went on.

"What does that mean?" Rae asked.

"I don't know," Demeter replied. "Look at this terrible mess!"

We were helping Demeter clean up when we saw the beat-up suitcase on the kitchen table.

"What do you think is in there?" I asked, pointing to the suitcase. I wasn't sure I really wanted to know. Strange shapes bulged out of its sides. Bits of stuff that looked like seaweed poked out from the edges. Why had the strange woman left it here?

Chapter 4

Exploring the Suitcase

Demeter drew a deep, nervous breath as she clicked open the lock on the suitcase.

"Careful," I warned. Who knew what might pop out?

Slowly, Demeter raised the top. Rae and I jumped back, but nothing happened.

"It looks like a bunch of junk," Rae said. "What is all this stuff?"

Demeter picked up a crinkly silver bag from the suitcase and read the label, "Instant walnuts. Just add water."

A piece of a torn brown bag was stuck to the back. There was writing on it. I peeled it off and read, "For the squirrels. They forget where their nuts are hidden."

Rae pulled a rain bonnet from the suitcase. It also had a note on it. "You will get wet," she read, "so you'll need this rain bonnet."

Then Demeter took a box about the size of an alarm clock from the suitcase. Suddenly the box began to ring loudly.

Demeter pushed a button on the box, then gasped. "It's her. It's that woman again!"

Rae and I looked over her shoulder. The white-haired woman's face smiled at us from inside the box. It looked as if she was on the world's smallest, handheld TV.

All of us jumped at once when the box started talking. "Welcome to the Mother Nature Alert Box," it said.

Then the woman began to talk. "You must
have known this was coming," she said. "After
all, your name *is* Demeter."

"What does she mean about your name?"
Rae wanted to know.

Demeter explained, "In ancient Greek myths,
or stories, Demeter was a kind of Mother Nature.
The ancient Greeks believed she controlled the
seasons. They believed that she made the plants
grow and the seasons change. They believed she
even controlled the weather. When it was stormy,
they thought Demeter was angry."

"That is like Mother Nature," I pointed out.

Demeter nodded glumly. "I learned all the
Greek stories about Demeter in school. I didn't
really think much about it being my name, too.
I figured my parents just liked it."

Now the woman on the screen was speaking again, "Anyway, being Mother Nature is a full-time job," she went on. "You are on duty 24/7. That means 24 hours a day, seven days a week! It's fun though, once you get used to it."

"Sure, I bet," Demeter grumbled.

The woman went on. "That tornado gave you all your powers. It spun them right in when it spun around you," she said.

"This is too unbelievable!" Demeter mumbled. "It can't be happening!"

"By the time you hear this I'll be off water skiing in Hawaii," the woman said. "I've earned this time off and now it's your turn. Good luck." The TV screen went blank.

Demeter sat down in a chair, lost in thought. She drummed her fingers on the table.

Suddenly she shot up from her chair. "No," she said firmly. "No! No! No!"

27

"What do you mean, no?" I asked.

"This is crazy. I am NOT Mother Nature," Demeter insisted. "Mother Nature is just an idea. She's not a real person. I'm a painter, and I have an art show to get ready. I can't possibly be Mother Nature. I don't have time."

Just then the phone rang. Demeter picked it up and barked into the receiver, "This is Demeter! *I* am Demeter Dunn!"

We could barely hear the tinny-sounding voice on the other end. "Why of course you are Demeter Dunn. You are also my favorite painter!" the voice said.

Demeter's angry face relaxed. Whoever it was, she seemed happy to hear from him. "Oh, hello, Mr. Delbart," she said in a friendly voice. "How are you?"

She covered the phone with one hand and spoke to us. "I'm sorry, Sam and Rae, I have to take this call. It's the owner of the gallery where my show is going to be."

"OK," Rae said, "we'll see you later." Rae and I headed back toward the front door.

I stopped in the living room to look at the seed painting again. "I still don't understand this kind of art," I admitted to Rae.

"It's modern art," Rae said. "It . . ." Whatever she was about to say was cut short by the sound of Demeter's angry voice.

"I hope you're joking!" we heard her shout. She sounded very upset.

"You want more pink in the show?" she said angrily. "I don't have pink paintings! You've seen my work. There's hardly any pink at all! In fact, I hate the color pink!"

/ I checked the paintings. She was right about one thing; there was hardly a speck of pink.

"I don't care if you have pink walls!" she yelled. "You can't ask an artist to start using pink just to match your walls!"

Demeter sounded angrier and angrier with every word she spoke. "Listen, Mr. Delbart, I've had a strange day and I'm not in the best mood. This is too much. Pink! Pink!" We could hear Demeter banging things around in her kitchen.

"What do you think? Do you think I can just wave my hand and make everything pink?" she exploded. "Fine. Go ahead. Make it pink!"

I turned to say something to Rae, but she was staring out the window with an astonished expression on her face. Rae's mouth was open. She was frozen with amazement.

I looked to see what she was staring at.
Suddenly I was frozen with amazement, too. I
had never seen anything like it in my whole life.

Chapter 5

Living in a World Gone Plaid

Everything had turned pink! The trees, the grass, the clouds—they were all pink!

"No, Mr. Delbart, I simply refuse," Demeter spoke on the phone. "There will be no pink! None!"

Poof! All the pink disappeared. Even the pink tulips in Demeter's yard were no longer pink. They were now gray.

"You might as well ask me for plaid!" Demeter exploded at Mr. Delbart.

Rae clutched my arm. Everything outside had turned plaid! Demeter's lawn looked like a long, plaid scarf. Her trees had plaid leaves on plaid branches. A plaid squirrel buried a plaid acorn in the plaid lawn. The gray tulips were plaid!

Rae and I stared at each other, wide-eyed. Demeter was making this happen. She really was Mother Nature!

Someone was sure to notice all this plaid outside. We had to tell Demeter about it so she could change it back right away. We ran to the kitchen, but Demeter held up her hand to stop us. She was still arguing with Mr. Delbart.

As she spoke into the phone, her voice grew even louder. "What do you mean you want everything tomorrow?" she cried. "I was supposed to have two full weeks to finish, Mr. Delbart. You're really making me angry now."

Lightning flashed. Thunder boomed. Rae and I hurried to the window. Outside, plaid trees tossed in an angry wind. Demeter was controlling the weather. The whole plaid world was storming angrily because Demeter was angry. We had to make her see what was happening!

Rae and I pulled Demeter to the window. She blinked hard; then she dropped the phone. "Hey!" Mr. Delbart yelled from the floor. No one paid any attention to him.

"What's going on?" Demeter gasped.

"You did that!" Rae told her. "When you said pink, everything turned pink. When you said no pink, the pink disappeared and everything turned gray. When you said plaid, everything turned plaid. When you said you were angry, the storm began. YOU made it happen!"

Demeter shook her head and moved away from the window. "This isn't happening. It can't be! I must be cracking up. That's it. I've been working too hard, and I need a rest. I have to lie down right away. See you later, kids."

That night, the TV news ran a special report. "Our town has gone plaid!" the reporter said.

Aunt Sue sat with us as we watched. The TV reporter interviewed a woman holding a plaid flower. "My garden is ruined!" she wailed.

"What happened?" Aunt Sue asked.

"It was an accident," Rae told her. "Demeter Dunn just became the new Mother Nature. She, uh, isn't really used to her new job yet."

"Is that so?" Aunt Sue said absent-mindedly.

"Yes," Rae babbled on, "she said 'make it plaid' by mistake."

"Well, well," Aunt Sue said. I could tell she wasn't really listening to Rae. Maybe that was a good thing.

The storm stopped. "Maybe Demeter calmed down," I whispered, "or fell asleep."

"That sounds like a good idea," Rae said as she yawned. "I'm going to sleep myself."

I went to bed, too. I lay there thinking about all the amazing things that had happened that day. Finally, I fell asleep. When I opened my eyes again, bright light streamed into my bedroom window. I couldn't believe I'd slept so late.

Turning, I checked my clock. It was four o'clock in the morning. "Four A.M.?" I mumbled, rubbing my eyes.

I sat bolt upright! "Wait a minute!" I cried. "It can't be this bright at four in the morning! What's going on here?"

Chapter 6

Demeter's Powers

I rushed down to the kitchen to see if anyone was up. Rae was sitting at the table, rubbing her eyes. "My clock must have stopped. It says four in the morning," she mumbled, "but it must be later than that."

That explained it! "We had a power outage during the night," I said, laughing. "I thought Demeter had done it again."

It turned out there was a perfectly normal explanation. What a relief!

Rae turned on the TV. It worked, so we knew the power was back on. She put on the weather channel, which also gave the time. The announcer said, "Our unusual plaid weather seems to have cleared up. Today's forecast is warm and sunny. The time is 4:10 A.M."

We looked at each other. "Uh oh," Rae said.

"It's Demeter!" we both cried. The power hadn't failed after all. Somehow Demeter had made the sun come up early. We hurried to the window and saw Demeter on her porch. She was painting in her bathrobe.

We quickly put on our sneakers and ran down the hill. When we reached her porch, Demeter looked up. "Hi, Rae. Hi, Sam. I had the strangest dream last night. You two were in it."

She placed her paintbrush at the bottom of her easel. "I dreamed I was Mother Nature. In my dream, I turned all of nature plaid. You can't imagine what it looked like! Everything was plaid. Isn't that funny? I woke up on this beautiful morning and just had to paint that dream," Demeter went on. "Hey, you two are still in your pajamas, too!" she added.

"Demeter, listen," Rae began. "It really is—"

"What time is it, anyway?" Demeter interrupted. "I was so eager to start painting I never noticed the time."

"Demeter, it's four o'clock in the morning," Rae told her.

"Oh, nonsense!" Demeter cried. "Look at how sunny it is. Surely it's later than four."

"No!" Rae continued. "The sun came up because you woke up. You made it happen."

"You are Mother Nature," I joined in. "This proves it!"

"Are you two trying to say that it wasn't a dream?" Demeter asked.

"It's real!" Rae cried. "When you were angry, it stormed. Now you're awake, the sun is up."

"Very funny," Demeter said, waving her hand. "You can't fool me that easily." She opened her front door and held it for us to enter.

"We're not kidding!" I insisted.

"Sure," she said. "If I were really Mother Nature, I could just point at those plants there and say 'Grow!' and they'd all start growing, right?"

As she spoke, she pointed at a row of potted plants on her windowsill. The plants looked brown and droopy, as if they hadn't been watered in a long time.

Then a streak of green light shot from Demeter's finger. It made a sizzling sound as it zapped the plants. POW! The plants turned green and healthy.

Then they began sprouting new growth everywhere. Leaves covered the walls and the window. Thick stems curled across the ceiling and wrapped around the furniture.

In seconds, Demeter's living room had turned into a jungle! Now we could hear animal sounds. Tree frogs croaked! Parrots chattered! Insects buzzed!

"It's a rain forest in here!" Rae cried.

A large parrot swooped into the room. It landed on Demeter's shoulder. "Mother!" it squawked.

"I'm not your mother!" Demeter snapped.

"Mother!" the parrot repeated.

Rae and I laughed.

Suddenly we heard a familiar ringing sound. It was the Mother Nature Alert Box. The three of us looked around to see where it was.

I spotted it first. It was tucked in the crook of a banana tree right behind me. Two lizards slithered away as I reached over to pick it up.

I held it while Demeter and Rae looked over my shoulder. Writing flashed across the little screen inside. "MOTHER NATURE NEEDED IN ARIZONA DESERT," the screen said.

"What now?" Demeter wondered.

Suddenly a strange feeling came over me. It was like pins and needles through my whole body. When I looked at my hand, it was glowing!

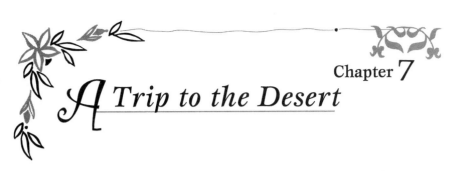

Chapter 7

A Trip to the Desert

Now I could see my entire body glowing. Then I must have blinked. The next thing I knew, I was standing alone in a desert.

Two glowing lights popped up next to me. Demeter and Rae stepped out of them. Rae's eyes were wide open. Demeter was just the opposite. Her eyes were tightly closed.

"This is not happening," Demeter said. Her eyes were still scrunched shut. Then she covered them with both hands and said, "This is not happening."

Rae and I looked at each other. We'd seen enough strange things already. Once you've seen a plaid squirrel, it's not that hard to believe you've been zapped into the desert. This was really happening, but why?

"Look," Rae cried, "baby deer!"

I looked where Rae was pointing. Sure enough, there were two fawns, each one lying in a kind of nest on the ground. They weren't baby deer, though.

Now I was the one who had trouble believing what was happening. "This is amazing," I told Rae. "These must be baby Sonoran pronghorn antelopes. Do you know how rare they are here? They're on the endangered species list!" I had seen a program on TV about the pronghorn antelope in Arizona's Sonoran Desert.

The fawns looked as if they were sleeping. I didn't see their mother anywhere around, but I knew pronghorn antelope were very fast runners. She was probably nearby.

"Their mother must have gone for food or something," I said.

Demeter finally opened her eyes. "What's that noise?" she asked.

Rae turned around. "Uh oh," she moaned.

The noise was the wind. This particular wind belonged to a big black cloud headed straight toward us.

This was too much for Demeter. She began to cry. "First a strange woman ruins my life," she wailed. "Then I get yanked out of my nice, comfortable house into the middle of a desert," she went on. "Now we're all going to get attacked by a dust storm." She spun around and began wildly waving her hands in the air. "I can't take it anymore!" she screamed.

As soon as she waved her hands, the dust storm changed course.

"You did it!" Rae yelled. "You saved an endangered species!"

This only made Demeter cry harder. Now it began to rain in the desert. Then I heard a familiar ringing again and looked down at the Mother Nature Alert Box that was still in my hand.

"MOTHER NATURE! RED ALERT! ALASKA!"
it said, as rain splashed on its screen.

That tingling feeling came over me again.
Just like before, I began to glow. Rae and
Demeter glowed, too. ZAP! The three of us
popped up somewhere else.

It sure wasn't the desert. Snow was
everywhere! Somehow we were all now dressed
in heavy clothing. "I guess this is Alaska," Rae
mumbled from beneath her scarf.

"That's what the box said," I agreed. "I guess the red alert in the desert was what that dust storm would have done to the baby pronghorns. Where's the red alert here?"

"Everything looks OK to me," Demeter said as she looked around. "Ah! Breathe that fresh air!" she sighed. "This place is too beautiful to be in trouble. All I see is fresh clean snow, blue water, and that big oil tanker sitting out there on the ocean."

"What about those funny birds?" Rae asked. She pointed to some rocks by the water on which several birds were sitting. The birds were sort of chubby and looked a little bit like small penguins with red and yellow beaks. I thought they were cute.

"Puffins," I told them.

"Excuse me?" Demeter asked.

"Those birds are puffins," I explained. "I like to watch nature shows on TV."

"Here comes one of those puffy birds," Rae said. One of the birds hopped right toward us, looking as if it had something to tell us.

It flapped its black wings and squawked loudly. "Oh, my!" Demeter gasped. "I understood that! The bird just said, 'Thank goodness you're here!'"

"It did?" Rae asked. "I wonder why. Hey, look! It's leaving footprints."

It was true. The black footprints were easy to see on the white snow. The puffin waddled closer to Rae. Now we could see black goo dripping from the bird's feathers.

This bird looked like it was in big trouble. Could Mother Nature help?

Chapter 8

Demeter Takes Charge

The puffin squawked a series of short, quick sounds. Demeter listened and nodded.

"What did it say?" I asked.

"The black gooey stuff on it is oil," she reported. "It's leaking from the tanker, but the captain doesn't know. This is terrible!"

"It's messy," Rae agreed, "but what's so terrible about it?"

"When birds get oil on their feathers, they can't swim or fly properly," Demeter said. "If the oil gets in their mouths, it will poison them. Fish in this harbor must have already gotten some of this oil inside them. It will poison them, too. Then it will also poison any puffin that eats a contaminated fish. This is an environmental disaster area!"

Demeter stopped talking and blinked a few times. "Wow," she said, "I didn't know I knew all that. Suddenly the words just popped into my head and I knew they were true."

"Well, someone needs to do something fast," I said. "That oil is starting to wash up on shore." I pointed down. A wave lapped against the beach, leaving a dark, oily mark. This was really awful!

"Well, you're Mother Nature," Rae reminded Demeter. "Can't you do something?"

Demeter sighed and her breath rippled the oil. It lifted slightly, as if it were a blanket being lifted off the water.

"Did you see that?" Rae asked.

"I wonder," Demeter said. "If my sigh can do that, I wonder what would happen if . . ."

She didn't finish her sentence. Instead, she took in a long, strong breath of air. Then she blew. The layer of black oil lifted in a single sheet. Demeter kept blowing. She was like a human wind storm.

The oil layer hung in the air for a second; then it landed on the tanker. Now the tanker looked as if it had been dipped in black paint. We heard a siren go off on the ship.

"Great!" Rae shouted.

"Way to go!" I cried.

Demeter grinned at us. "Not bad, if I do say so myself. Now they'll notice what's going on with their tanker and patch that leak."

At that moment, an official-looking truck
bumped along over the snow toward us. It
stopped and two people in uniforms got out.
"How did you get here?" one of them asked.

"Do you realize that tanker out there is
leaking oil?" Demeter asked back.

"How do you know that?" the other person
wanted to know. Then she looked out at the
gooey black tanker.

"Oh, no! We'd better report this right away," the man said. He jumped back into the truck. The woman got into the driver's seat and started the engine. The man began punching buttons on a walkie-talkie as the truck quickly sped away.

"Wow, for a minute there I thought we were in big trouble," I said.

"If anyone's going to be in trouble, it's that oil company," said Demeter firmly. "How could they be so careless? How could they ruin nature's beauty and hurt its creatures?"

Demeter struck a pose; then she started to make a speech. "Nature is so important," she said. "When something hurts a part of nature, it hurts all of us." It looked as if Demeter was ready to go on all day. Then a familiar ringing came from Demeter's pocket.

Chapter 9

A Painted Desert

The box whooshed us back to the desert. This time the problem was easy to find.

"Oh, no!" Demeter cried. "I forgot to turn off the rain. I've flooded the desert!" It wasn't exactly flooded. It was just very, very wet.

"This rain must stop!" Demeter shouted.

The rain stopped. I couldn't believe it. The sun came out and began to dry up the water.

"Thank goodness," Demeter said with a sigh as she sat down on a flat rock.

"You're getting good at this," Rae told her.

"How can you say that?" Demeter asked. "If I'd really been paying attention, maybe I could have prevented that oil leak. Look how I nearly turned this desert into a swamp."

As she spoke, I saw something strange going on. Flowers were popping out of the cactus plants, and there were animals everywhere.

"I've heard about this," Rae said. "It's the desert after a rainstorm. It blooms, and the animals come out to eat the plants and drink the water. Look at this cactus flower!"

Demeter walked over to the flower and studied it for a moment. "The color is lovely, but the overall effect is rather dull, I think. If I were painting this flower, I'd give it red stripes," she said. Suddenly, the flower had red stripes.

A slow smile spread across Demeter's face and her eyes sparkled. She turned to a white cactus flower and said, "I'd give this one blue spots." Suddenly, the flower had blue spots.

"How would you like a rainbow?" she asked happily. She didn't wait for our answer. She swung her arm overhead and a many–colored arc streaked across the sky. *This is great!* I thought. I had never seen anything so beautiful.

"This is such fun!" Demeter shouted. "I thought being Mother Nature meant I had to stop being a painter. It doesn't mean that at all. Now I have the biggest canvas ever! I can paint the whole wide world!"

"I think she's finally getting into it," Rae said with a smile.

I nodded. "It sure looks that way."

Soon the Mother Nature Alert Box rang again. This time it zapped us back where we had started, in Demeter's kitchen. While we were gone, the rain forest had disappeared.

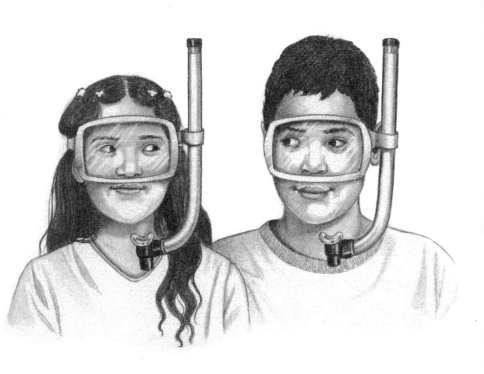

Demeter gazed out her kitchen window, smiling. "Wait until you see the autumn leaves once I get through with them this fall," she said.

"I can't wait," Rae told her.

The Mother Nature Alert Box beeped again. Demeter showed us the message: CORAL REEF IN DANGER.

Demeter took snorkel masks from the beat-up suitcase that the old Mother Nature had left and handed one to each of us. "Ready?" she asked with a big smile.

I turned to Rae. "Can you believe it?" I said. "How could I have ever thought this summer was going to be boring?"

*G*lossary

abstract   [AB strakt] not realistic

boredom   [BOR dum] a state of feeling that something is dull or uninteresting

contaminated   [kun TAM ihn ayt ed] made dirty or infected by touching it or mixing it with materials that are harmful

convertible   [kun VURT ih bul] a car with a removable roof

environmental   [en VYE ruhn ment uhl] describing things that surround anything, especially all the conditions that surround a person, animal, or plant, and affect growth

galleries   [GAL uh reez] places that display and sell art

official   [uh FIHSH ul] coming from someone in charge

raved   [rayvd] praised greatly

retire   [rih TYR] to give up one's work, business, or career

somersault   [SUM ur sawlt] to roll the body over head first, with heels following